Blue Highways
by Shelly Cole

Pencil Drawings by Ella Spice
Cover Art by Nick Holmes

TABLE OF CONTENTS

For Monkey, my truest Love, my best friend,
the beginning and end of every day.
Without even trying, you have created the
corner of our own world.

PROLOGUE: Nick Holmes

Shelly:

An armored car with a stained-glass
windshield.

A razor on a pillow.

A hollow-point multi-vitamin.

On a highway crawling with coyotes. ...no
need to rush along - better we howl
together a while. True north is here
somewhere.

Making hurt make some kind of sense is a
custom forged brand of reason and strength.
I'm not sure I understood the stab wound of
a single sigh until I watched a lover drive
away in anger. Forgot my own birthday.
Kids these days.

For certain I fell in love with Shelly's mind.
With this human. With honesty. And she's
always honest.
A pleasure to be brought to attention with
this prose.

Shelly is a phoenix. An artist of un-killable devotion. A selfless teacher. A gallery of femininity as well as a brute force reminder of what it means to be kind.

Enjoy these tales for their candor and rhythm. It's bold and brave to have someone let you in like she's done with this collection. Deeply personal and recounted with style.

Raise your hand and go first. Learn from her - someone who has done so with ferocity for joy.

Life pays you back occasionally; it's a wonderful kind of privilege to know this human. Now you get to also, if only a little.

Thank you Shelly. For sharing and loving. It's a better world.

PART ONE: A GUIDE TO BEATING THE BULLIES

STEP ONE: Know when to admit defeat.

STEP TWO: When someone just needs a hug.

How do I start? Where do I begin? What is the story among all of these stories that should be the first one to tell? And really, what is the point after all? I lived it. I lived every day thinking, this is life, I guess. Who really knows what a normal childhood should be? Who.

As the 60's gave way to the 70's and then 70's had their way, drugs, fashion, divorce and opioids touched the coming generation. Well, my story starts in that weird space where no one spoke of and the kids seemed to die, emotionally. No one talks about it because it was the in-between time. Baby-boomer baby meets welcome to the party.

Trial and error, the story my life. And where did I get the grace to keep trying.

STEP THREE: Listen.

STEP FOUR: Tell your stories. They mean something.

When I was 9 and I didn't know what was wrong or what was right, and I stood in the doorway of their bedroom wondering what I was looking at. And as he invited me in, I asked what those marks on his neck were. And so he asked me if I wanted to try, to see if i could give him the same marks my mother did, while she fried bacon one floor up. And when she walked in the room and laughed at me trying to do what she did, I felt so ashamed and I didn't understand any of it. He was naked under a sheet. And she had the bacon. And I felt so alone..

In the 70's and 80's the mom always got the children in a divorce. No one thought to ask who would take care of me. Who would wake me, feed me, tell me what to wear, give me a lunch, get me on the bus, make me bathe, help me understand math, tell me to go to sleep, protect me when the rats gnawed through my wall next to my bed and crawled across my body in the middle of the night. Or the rare glimpse of my "grandmother" swaying in my bedroom doorway, accusing me of sex when I was too

young to understand sex or why someone is
standing in my doorway calling me a whore.

Who will listen? Who will say everything
is gonna be okay?
Maybe I should just put my head down and
get through it.

Until I couldn't anymore. Until I knew that
even though she would never forgive me,
she would tell me that I hurt her, that she
thinks that I am
leaving her, at 13,
because my dad was
giving me sex, even
though the only
thing I knew of sex
is what her own
mother yelled at
me years before,
drunk and swaying
in my bedroom
doorway,Sleeping
was rare because
rats were also my
cellmates.

No one believed me
when I told them. I didn't even know that I
wasn't safe.

PART TWO: THE FIRST TIME I SAW MY DAD CRY

My first and greatest Hero. Flawed. But never without love in his sweet heart.

I was five years old and living in rural Oklahoma. He took me out into the woods that surrounded my house. He brought a BB gun, to teach me how to aim a weapon. He was in the Vietnam War. He knew his way around a gun. We saw a little bird. He told me to watch, that he was going to shoot the dirt next to the birdy. "Just to scare her." He took aim. I stopped breathing. I was so scared. He fired. He shot the birdy. He killed her. I cried. When he saw me cry he filled with shame. My Hero. It was like seeing Santa Clause, sidled up to the bar, cigarette in one hand, whiskey in the other.

And on the worst day, many years later, well after he was diagnosed with Bipolar One, upon finding him patrolling the parking lot of his apartment building, wearing only underwear, and toting a shotgun. "Dad, dad? Please come inside. What are you doing? It's 3:00 in the mornin' and, well it's cold out here."

"It's okay Shell, I gotta keep us safe."

"But Daddy, you
gotta put some
clothes on. Yer
scarin' the
neighbors. Daddy
give me the
shotgun okay.
Please? Dad?"

"GET IN THE
FOXHOLE
SOLDIER, GET
DOWN!"

"Okay Daddy,
okay. I'm down... Okay sir, let me take a turn
at watch. You rest for a little and I'll keep
us safe. You done a good job. A real good job.
Time to rest. Yeah, okay good... good job
soldier... I love you Daddy. I'm right here,
I'm not going anywhere."

PART THREE: DEFINE CRAZY

I found peace outside of my mother. I found
out that my father needed me. As I grew
into my 20's I realized, I came to truly
understand bipolar disease and I spent
decades understanding and managing my
father's illness. On my own. It's lonely
taking care of someone all alone. It's
exhausting explaining to doctors who don't
understand and begging them to listen to
me, and please don't give him anti-
depressants and oh why did you do that
because now look what he is. He thinks he's a
brain surgeon and a green beret and he's
suffering and he doesn't understand what is
happening to him and I'm the only one who
understands and I'm so tired of explaining it
and can I just get a break?!

Finally he found a place to lay down. And
got medicine. And the nurses knew that
visiting hours didn't apply to me as I got
him settled, got him stable, sleeping on
folding chairs in his hospital room for weeks
as I helped him to feel safe in the hospital.

Now. Who takes care of me? Where is my
home? What's real? What's worth telling?
How did I survive?

Telling the stories about my mother, or her teenage lover who watched me shower and laughed at my naked body, not understanding why he was there, and why she let him, or why my brother did what he did, why I feel so alone now after all of it. I did survive.

Reading, drugs, sleeping, hiding, making friends, taking too many risks, watching my dad die slowly and loving my dad every moment of my life.

FLASHBACK: West Covina County Mental Hospital 2006 I was broken, Jack was with me. 72 hours.

Hello. I'm Jack. I'm Shelly's stuffed bunny. I've been with her my whole life, except at the very beginning when I was at the factory being made for her. We've had a lot of good days. And maybe a few bad ones. We're going to tell you about our 3 days at the West Covina County Psychiatric Hospital. We met some pretty wild people there. Our roommate. She was an old Russian woman who never left the room. She slept all day with the covers pulled way up high, and she'd laugh like a nut and repeat over and again, "Hello Kitty. Hello Kitty." She walked the room all night long, back and forth, back and forth.

And Vanessa.

Vanessa, can I ask you a question? Why did you try to kill yourself? I don't know. I got a husband and a kid and a dead end job filing papers at a law firm. I just don't know where I belong. How old are you, Vanessa? I'm 20. Oh, well I just broke up with my boyfriend. Fuck guys. Yeah. Fuck em.

JACK: Can I tell them about Marcus? Yeah.

Marcus. He was our favorite person there. (whisper) He sold drugs. And he liked gangster rap. But he was real nice. I think he coulda probably done anything he wanted. He protected us once. In the lunch room, when Andrew, that thug, and Jane, the really old Korean woman that wore really tight spandex over her pot belly, They ganged up on Shelly. Jane screamed "Korean War Korean War" right in Shelly's face. I thought she was gonna punch Shelly. And Andrew, creepy middle-aged Andrew who reminded me of Shelly's gross "Stepfather Ted", ew, Andrew got right up in

her face, Baby Honey, listen you jest need to git yourself a man. Git a pretty bra and pretty panties
It went back and forth between the two,

and then . . .

BOOM! Marcus!

JACK: Oh man, he told them! HE STOOD UP ON THE TABLE!

Marcus: Listen up you animals, if anyone says another word to this little girl, Ima knock you on your ass!

JACK: He was not messing around.

ME: Jack, we saved the best for last.

JACK: THE JAR?

ME: Yep. Mr. Take-it-out-and-put-it-in-a-jar.

It took us a long time to understand what he was saying. Every day, through 3 group therapies. Breakfast Lunch and Dinner. He only ever said the same 9 words over and over, while grabbing the top of his head and

then clapping that hand into the one sitting
in his lap.

And then it became so clear. Please God,
please just take it out and put it in a jar so
that it can't hurt me anymore.

Heartbreaking.

And at the end of that 72 hours hold, to see
Kim's familiar face on the other side of the
locked door, I swore I would never end up in
a place like that, or in a state like that, ever
again.

PART FOUR: HEAVEN

When I discovered that Heaven was a place

to wait . . .

I was five when I asked my dad if he would
tell me about Heaven. I didn't understand
the idea of it and so he described it the best
he could. He said it was a place we go if
we're good. A place where we see all the
people who went before us. We get to be
with them again. And so I asked, "what do
we do there and are they waiting for us to
get there?" He said, yes, they'll be waiting
for me, just like he will. "And then what?" I
thought Heaven was a place we go to do
stuff, like run and play and laugh. But from
what I understood my dad to be saying, it
seemed to me that Heaven was a place we go
to wait. Wait for what? We wait for the
people we love to join us? And then what?
We keep waiting. I asked him how long does
Heaven last, and he replied, "forever."

It sacred me, this notion of waiting and
waiting for eternity. Because forever never
ends. I'll just be waiting and waiting and the

waiting never ends. It scared me to my core. Just the waiting.

It's when I had my first panic attack. I couldn't breathe, my heart raced, I didn't understand what was happening to me. Five year olds shouldn't have panic attacks. I hid in my closet and I cried and cried, thinking of sitting in limbo. Is that all there is to life? Then what's the point? What is the point?

I've come to understand, now, finally, that the point is to live as best I can. To give to others. To nurture and care for and foster those around me. To help those who hurt and to provide joy where I can. What else

is there?and to provide joy where I can. What else is there and to provide joy where I can. What else is there?and to provide joy where I can. What else is there?

PART FIVE: ALONE

I like to joke around and say, "When I was young and in school I was that weird girl in the corner."

But it's not really a joke. I have learned in my life so far that being alone is my constant. It's been my friend and my nemesis for nearly all of my life. At five years old when my kindergarten teacher was rearranging the seating chart she asked me where I wanted to sit.

I'd just returned from a long absence and she thought maybe I'd like to sit in the circle next to my only friend. But I didn't. I asked to drag my desk to the corner of the room and sit by myself. I always carried in my pocket the little dog from the Monopoly game and I felt that he was my only real friend.

My mother was an alcoholic. And as far as I could tell she always despised me. She hated me, as if she had a personal vendetta she owed me. I remember being 8, coming home from school, the first day of Christmas break. She was waiting for me in my bedroom. Sitting in a chair, the smell of alcohol filling the room, she didn't say anything. She just stared at me, trying to form words. Finally she said, "where have you been?" At school of course. Oh no, this is going to be a bad day. I was hiding something under my coat. A paper plate with a macaroni reindeer glued to it, and painted gold. My stupid gift for her. She asked me what I was hiding. "A surprise, mommy. Your Christmas present." "Give it to me," she screeched. "No mommy." She ripped it from my coat, took one look, laughed bitterly, threw it to the ground and staggered out of my room. I'll never understand why she hated me. But she always treated me that way, like a bother, like a pesky rodent she couldn't rid herself of. My only guess is that she was so hurt inside herself that it was just easier to put it on me. Thinking of her as a little hurt child gives me the courage to (at least try) to forgive her.

But the horror of her abuse towards me didn't end with her. She allowed her creepy husband Ted to abuse me as well. I can't talk about that stuff. It's too much. I was 8 when my parents divorced. I was forced to live with them until, finally at 13, I had the courage to tell her that I was leaving.

Going to live with my dad, who would care
for me and give me a safe place for at least
the next 4 years. To go to the same school.
To make friends. To eat breakfast and have
lunch money and an actual dinner rather
than the pot of beans that we ate every
night with ketchup because all of her
money, the money my dad paid her for child
support, went to vodka and cigarettes.
I moved to 9 different schools in the 5 years
I lived with her. I was the weird girl who
sat alone in her dirty clothes, hungry. I
think of that little girl now and my heart
breaks for her.

And I share this with the children I teach,
so that they can know that if they are that
weird kid who sits in the corner too, that I
understand. And that it got better for me.

Alone means something different now. I
have no relatives. I haven't since my dad
died in 2004. But now, instead of the little
Monopoly dog, I have my Monkey dog. She is
always by my side and she is with me in
nearly every dream I have. She is my
constant.

I look around and I see that alone looks
different now.

Now I have friends, people who love me,
take care of me, laugh with me and will be
there whenever I ask for help or company.
And I've had to learn that it's okay to ask
for help.

I'm not afraid of being alone anymore. What
I hope for is my own corner of the world,
with a family of my own. A family of Three.
And friends. And students that I love, that
I will listen to and laugh with and take
care of in any way I can.

What I know is this: people leave. They
always leave. By way of death,
betrayal, a change of heart, vacation, or
perhaps a hundred other reasons. And I
know now that if I can be alone and feel
safe with myself then I can be the best
version of myself for the world around me.
And maybe I can have that family of my
own.

PART SIX: PRIDE

My first crush, Morgan McMillan. Black hair,
smiling eyes. 10 years old. One of the many
brief school stops in my young life. It was
Track and Field Day. The school was tiny.
Somehow, I was assigned a team captain and
we chose our teams by one-at-a-time picking
from all of the kids standing in a large
crowd. I went first. I picked Morgan. Oh! He
was so hot. Or, as my 10 year old self: so
dreamy. I constructed a fierce team,
including Russel, the largest boy of the
bunch, who kids made fun of because he sat
alone, hunched over, and in the corner. He
really came through for us in the Tug-of-
War. I aced the obstacle course and when I
passed the finish line, Morgan gave me wink
and a thumbs up. I could have melted onto
the field right then and there.

The day ended and we were the winningest
team in the entire middle school. I went
home that day feeling so loved and I
carried it with me as, soon after, we moved
on to the next town.

PART SEVEN: GOD, part one

I've experienced the presence of God exactly
twice in my life. The first time was after
my dad died. He took a long time to die.
Emphysema. I was living in Los Angeles. He
was in a Veterans hospital in a small town
in Texas, outside of Austin. Often, I would
get the call from his doctor: "You better get
here. He's not going to make it through the
weekend." And I so would go. Always on the
first plane out. This went on for about a
year. My dad was bed-ridden, unable to
walk. Atrophy had set in. All he had was his
window, his television, the kindness of his
nurses, and me. It was on my last visit to
see him when his doctor pulled me out of his
hospital room and into the hallway. "We
need to talk about your father's endgame.
You see, every time he gets pneumonia we
medicate him, and then you get here, and he
bounces back. It's time to stop."

And he decided that it was up to me to tell
my dad. The hard part. Two
songs got me through this time. The Flaming
Lips' "Do You Realize" and Blur's "Sweet
Song." Time to do the second hardest thing
of my life. He was so afraid. He didn't want
to die. And I didn't want to be the one to

tell him it was time. But I did. My sweet daddy. Yes, he was a lot of work. A constant worry in my life. So many times sitting on my closet floor and crying because I felt so alone in the taking care of him. Of never knowing what he was going to do next. Who would call me late in the night to tell me what he'd done. In and out of mental hospitals my entire adult life. Being his legal guardian and having to make that terrible decision each time I had to put him back in. He hated it in there. I did too, during my brief time in the West Covina County Hospital. Sometimes it was downright funny, the things he did. Funny, in a not-funny-at-all-but-it-feels-better-to-laugh kind of way. Like heading into his favorite bar, where the bartender had me on speed dial. Him, wearing hospital scrubs, a stethoscope, a pager, and fake blood smeared all over his scrubs. His pager goes off. He uses the payphone. He returns, broken and crying, "I just lost a patient."

Dad, what are you most afraid of, if you let go? He said he was most afraid of there being nothing else, of this being it. And if he leaves this, then he will just cease to exist. He asked me what I thought. I said, "Dad, I'd like to believe there's something else. But I just don't know for certain, in my heart."

It was time to move to the hospice unit on the 5th floor. He hated that idea. So I went upstairs, found the head nurse and begged her to give my dad his own room, with a view, because after all, he can't walk. All he has are the clouds. She said she can't guarantee anything. But she agreed to come meet him later that day. She kept her promise. She sat by his bed as I stood by the window. She cooed to him about how wonderful it was on the fifth floor. Conspiratorially, she told him how the nurses were so much sweeter and prettier up there. And she promised him his own room, with a window that overlooked the most beautiful grove of trees and how the sky went on forever. I think, after seeing how little time he had left, she knew it was an easy promise. The next morning, I said goodbye, knowing that it would be the last time. And knowing that he would never be able to let go of this life in my presence. I'm crying as I write this.

The job of being his daughter was a great and fierce pleasure.

Two nights later, hours after I had hung up
the phone with him, I awoke with a knowing
that he had gone. I laid awake until the sun
came up, quietly saying my goodbye. At 7am,
the phone rang. That night was the first
time I understood that there is something
more than this physical life on earth. I
knew because he came to tell me the answer
to his own question. And to say Goodbye...
Goodbye Daddy. I miss you every day.

PART EIGHT: GOD, part two

There was a deer outside my window.

Let me back up.

After about 5 years of living in Denver, in the midst of a difficult situation, I moved in with the family of one of my beloved students, Amanda. They saved my life when they opened their home to me. Really, it was the first time I ever felt like I was part of a real, functioning family.

My room was in the walk-out basement where there was a koi pond.
Outside my bedroom window there was a dirt area underneath the upstairs deck. It cleared about 4 feet and getting underneath that deck was very tricky. I'll come back to that.

I love animals. Anyone who knows me knows this. My heart aches for animals. In any movie, I don't care who you kill but don't kill an animal. I can't even watch wildlife specials because I can't take watching the lion take down the gazelle. I weep.

So we come home from somewhere, and this place where we lived, it was a wildlife preserve in a forest of rolling hills. There were bears, bobcats, wildcats, turkeys and deer. As we pulled up the drive and I opened the car door, Monkey leapt out and ran right up to a deer in the yard. And the deer just stood there. She didn't move. When I got closer, trying to grab Monkey, I saw that the deer's back right leg looked like it has passed through a meat grinder. And Amanda said she saw a coyote run away when Monkey charged at them. And then slowly the deer turned around and walked into the woods.

In this gated community where we lived there are security guards and so we called and they sent out two guys, one older and kind, the other a young punk I wanted to punch in the testicles. I was crying and the younger guy was trying to hide his laughter, while the older fellow was attempting to comfort me. They tried to find her. And the man told me what was likely to happen was that she would find her herd and the buck would take care of her. That he would chew through the sinew and the bone and amputate her leg.

I thought, there is no chance of that and I was certain she was a goner.

A couple of months later I heard Monkey barking in my room. When I went to investigate I found her at the base of the window barking at a deer peering into my room. She stood there a long time, just looking at me. I pulled out my phone and took her picture. Then she took a few more steps. Her back right leg was amputated and what remained was only a stump. Shocked, I caught my breath, snapped another photo and stood there in awe. I believe she came

to thank Monkey for chasing that coyote off and saving her life. And she came to tell me that she was okay. And for me, that was God.

PART NINE: "YOU CAN'T PEE IN AN ANTIQUE TOILET, PRAIRIE WHORE!"

There is an old Civil War Fort in Fernandina, Florida called Fort Clinch, named after General Duncan Lamont Clinch. Clinch garnered fame after General Andrew Jackson ordered him to attack Fort Negro, which was an instigating factor in the Second Seminole War. Fort Negro was set up by British Forces as a safe haven for escaped slaves. His attack was viewed a success, as hundreds of Seminoles and slaves died.

Just after my first visit to the VA hospital that my dad had been admitted to (the beginning of his last year alive) I left exhausted and depleted. I'd spent 6 days sleeping on folding chairs in his hospital room. It was my job to educate the doctors and nurses caring for him. They didn't know he was Bipolar and that he NEEDS TO BE MEDICATED! He was a lot, to say the least, and the nurses were ripping their hair out trying to care for him. In a wheelchair, 100% manic, awake all hours of the day and night, pressing his call button practically nonstop and screaming at everyone, I'm surprised they didn't put a pillow over his head and snuff him out. As for me, I got zero sleep and I staggered out of that hospital and onto a plane that took me to a very welcome respite in Florida, visiting my best friends Michael and Kevin. We stayed in the RV that was parked on the front lawn of Michael's parents' house in the woods, and surrounded by plastic flamingoes and lawn chairs. Back in those days we all had a lot more money than sense, and we guzzled bottles of Veuve Clicquot while driving around Amelia Island, Florida. The relief I felt to be out of the VA trenches and drunk on good champagne was unforgettable and saved me from falling into a deep well of sadness. Having my dad as my only "real" family was pushing me towards the depths of loneliness. And having Michael and Kevin as my brothers during that excruciating time is a gift I will always be grateful for. On one of those drunken days we visited Fort Clinch State Park. In the gift shop on the way into the Fort the boys purchased a bonnet that they insisted I wear, not just during our tour of the Fort, but for the rest of our stay in Florida, and then on to The Hamptons and then New York City. From that day forward I will always be known as The Prairie Whore. And when a prairie whore has to pee, she pees in an antique toilet on display at an old Southern Civil Ward Fort. As I thought of all the murdering of slaves and Seminoles that General Clinch was responsible for, it felt like a choice that I could stand behind.

During that time in my life I was madly in love with a guy named Alexis. Now, Alexis brought his own shipping container full of baggage. And breaking up with him nearly did me in. Cut to the West Covina County Hospital. But that would be a long time from now. Which leads me to...

PART TEN: THE BEST DANG NEW YEAR'S EVE LIKE, EVER!

2003. It was a beautiful and painful, stressful and celebratory fall. The film I had done that I was most proud of, Prey For Rock n Roll, was being well received, as it had its premiere at Sundance the previous spring. It was purchased at Sundance, and was now on tour throughout film festivals in the fall. I played the drummer Sally, and I kicked ass. (Thank you Malcolm Cross for breathing, bleeding and sweating in your effort to teach me, endure my screaming and flinging my sticks across the room in frustration, and eventually getting me to trust you enough to believe it when you said it would all click into place.) As our film was touring, they hired a punk band to accompany it on its way. And he was the drummer. I met him upstairs after the first show at The Hard Rock on Sunset Boulevard. As the party got underway, I was riding very high on life. He bumped into me in the crowd, turned around and recognition filled his face. He said, "You're Shelly, the drummer!" My breath caught. I was immediately filled with the certainty that I was meeting the most exactly perfect person that the Universe had in store for me. And I hadn't even known I was waiting for him until just that moment.

But as I said, Alexis brought a kind of stress on my life that triggered levels of fear and abandonment I may never recover from. It wasn't his fault. Not entirely. He was just never able to offer me the kind of home in his heart that I have always needed. My own corner of the world.

For me, I found that my friendships with a handful of the men in my life have endured all of the trials that most of my Los Angeles girlfriends were unable to weather. These boys just brought out the best in me. Never judged me. Always laughed. And who are all still securely in place as my family. Maybe it's because we didn't talk about the bad stuff all that much. They knew it was there, but rather than focusing on it, we spent our time having adventures.

And it was after this crazy fall that we went to New York City and spent our New Year's Eve in a loft at the top of the Flatiron Building, belonging to a well-known Broadway musical director. They had bin after bin of costumes... And, of course, cases and cases of Veuve (did I mention I LOVE

VEUVE?) Right after the stroke of midnight our host led us all into the dance studio and asked us to find a costume, and that we were going to put on a fabulous fashion show! Kevin donned a fur Russian Babushka hat and full mink stole. With his pants pulled down around his ankles, he strode the runway in one of the most genius makeshift costumes I have ever seen. The mood was perfect. The laughter was effortless. I thought, "I could die right now and I could die happy."

The next morning, out for a stroll, as the snow fell on our sleepy faces and tucked under
Alexis'
arm, I
turned my
chin up
and asked
him, "Do
you love
me?" And
he replied,
"I do,
Prairie
Whore. I sure do."

What a way to break my heart.

PART ELEVEN: WHEN CRYSTAL METH IS NOT THE ANSWER

I was at the tender age of twenty. In art school studying photography.
Trying desperately to understand my father's madness. Having fling after fling.
Feeling lost. Scared. Alone. I had yet to discover acting, which became the savior of my life.

At eighteen I read a book, Siddhartha by Herman Hesse. Siddhartha journeyed all over the world searching for the meaning of life. It was only after returning to his childhood village as a very old man, that he understood. As he watched his old friend Govinda sit by the river and breathe in the smell of it, the simple beauty of it, he realized that the meaning of life was always right here, always within his reach, waiting for him to receive it. Should he choose to.

This was the beginning of my quest, my inward search, to find the elusive home that I would always feel safe in. On that search, I sampled many drugs along the way: acid, ecstasy, cocaine, weed, and, of course, crystal meth, the most disgusting invention of the human science lab. No one ever took a good look at "speed teeth" and said, "Now there's a good look." Thankfully I never got to that point. It was in the midst of coming down from a meth high that I realized, "If I don't get the f**k out of Texas I'm either going to die here, and soon, or I'll find myself in my mid-twenties with several children by several different men, and assistant managing a drive-through fast food chain.

So I chose to get the f**k out of Texas. I packed up everything I could take on a plane, wrapped up my 4.0 gpa semester, and took myself to only place outside of Texas that I knew someone: Seattle, Washington. During the Grunge Years. My friends all told me I was crazy and "you can't just pick up and move and leave everything behind!" But I did.

It turned out to be one of the great decisions of my life. It's where I discovered acting.

Out of the blue I decided to audition for a play I saw on a flier at the local natural food store on Broadway Avenue in Capitol Hill. The play, called Scam America!, was

about four grifters who all come together
by various circumstances, and drive across
the country pulling scams. I auditioned for
the 16 year old grifter with a bad past and a
family she was running away from. I GOT A
CALLBACK! But after the callback the
director called me and said that, while I
was her first choice for the role, she just
couldn't cast me in such a huge role
considering the fact that I have never
acted before, didn't have a headshot and
resume, and that it was just took big a risk. I
was devastated. I took it pretty hard.
And then five days later she called me back.
She knew, that after a week's worth of
rehearsals with a seasoned Seattle
Repertory Theatre actor in the role, that
her instinct about me was right. That I was
the person to play that little girl grifter. I
worked hard for that director and her play.
And it was there that I discovered that
acting was it for me. It would be the thing
that carried me well into my twenties,
thirties and forties and save my life, has
given it meaning.

PART TWELVE: COUNTING NUMBERS

BECAUSE...

I'm a counter. I count in order to quell the
chaos in my mind. When I catch myself
counting especially fervently I know I'm
really going through a spell, and that the
chaos has grown out of control. If you're a
person who counts then you understand this
particular neurosis and how it manifests. I
often find myself saying "Shhh, it's okay" to
the little girl in my head. The little girl in
her closet who is afraid and just wants to be
held. I mean, we all want to be held right? I
do. I crave it. Touch. It helps me feel safe.

I talk about this chaos and counting quite
openly with my students in hopes that they
are encouraged to speak about their own
fears. I want them to know that it's okay.
Whatever it is, it's okay. And that, chances
are, the person sitting next to you is feeling
or has felt the same way at some point.

And that you are not alone.

You are not alone. We are all scared. We all
want to feel loved, understood and

accepted. We've all experienced bullying at some point in our lives. And I think we've all bullied to some extent, sometime in our lives. Maybe we still bully someone. Maybe we're still bullied by someone. The best we can do is show up for each other, allow our flaws to be seen. To be understood. To be able to apologize without making excuses.

PART FOURTEEN (BECAUSE THERE IS NO THIRTEEN): BIGGEST IRK

"I'm sorry but..." That's plenty out of you. I stopped listening.

THE FOLLOWING FEW STORIES ARE
NEITHER HERE NOR THERE. THEY ARE
JUST IMPORTANT TO ME. FEEL FREE TO
SKIP AHEAD.

PART FIFTEEN: ON HITCHHIKING

When I was 21 years old, and before I
moved to Los Angeles to begin my acting
career, I had a hippy boyfriend with a great
sense of adventure. We spent much of our
time in the mountainous rainforest of the
Olympic Peninsula. If you've ever been there
then you know. If you haven't, then here it
is: Have you ever seen the 1985 film Legend
starring Tom Cruise? It was like that. The
most magical forest, moss, mist and trickling
brooks. The cleanest air I've ever breathed
in. You may even spot a unicorn. Or maybe I
was just on mushrooms. It should be said
that I've only eaten mushrooms a handful of
times. And it's been decades since. But I
never had a bad time...
It was around this time that I discovered
Jack Kerouac and I could not get enough of
his writing, his philosophy, his utter
coolness. Damn he was cool. And in fact, that
year, instead of celebrating Christmas, I
celebrated Jack-mas. All things Jack. I

insisted that I would only accept Jack-
themed gifts and I spent Jack-mas in a tent
next to a stream and foraging for food.

I discovered the art of letting go.

And so, once again, I relinquished almost all
of my possessions and hit the road from
Seattle down the Texas.

Traveling the . . .

. . . BLUE HIGHWAYS

. . . through Washington State, Oregon,
Idaho, Utah, Colorado (got a tattoo in
Boulder), down to New Mexico and dropped
off at my friend's doorstep in Denton, Texas,
where I'd gone to college. Full Circle.

Did I almost get murdered along the way?
I'll never know. But I made it. And it was
cool. Took me two weeks of sleeping in a
tent just off the highway in whatever
gathering of trees I could find. This was the
early 90s. I wouldn't recommend this no

PART SIXTEEN: GROSS EXPECTATIONS

I categorize my life as before my mother/
after my mother. After my mother, at age
almost fourteen, was when my life began,
when I went to live with my dad. During
this time and on an obligatory visit to my
mother, I travelled on a Greyhound bus for
three hours. From Houston to where she
lived in a motel in Mesquite, Texas the bus
passed through Huntsville, where the state
penitentiary is housed.

And on this particular glowing Friday
evening a slew of just-released men, who
had clearly been drinking since the moment
they were let out, piled on the bus. One
particularly drunk fellow sloshed himself
down into the seat next to me, but sadly, did
not pass out. So as I was reading the same
paragraph over and over from Charles
Dickens' Great Expectations, this man
rambled on in a language so booze-garbled
that, had I lit a match, I think the whole
bus would have gone up in flames. It was the
part of the book where we are introduced to
Miss Havisham's dilapidated stone garden. It
was so bleak, so depressing. And after
reading that passage dozens of times for

fear of turning the page, it is seared into
my brain for life.

Finally, FINALLY, he got up to go to the
bathroom at the rear of the bus and I
immediately moved to the seat just behind
the driver. Maybe a half hour later I really
had to pee. And when I opened the door to
the bathroom I found him passed out on the
toilet, pants around his ankles, head resting
on the floor, the smell so toxic I nearly
threw up on him.

BACK TO THE POINT, IF THERE EVER WAS
ONE:

TO BE HELD. WHAT ELSE IS THERE?
I can only speak for myself when I say it's
the beginning and the end of everything.

TO BE LOVED. THERE'S NOTHING BETTER.
All I know is what I love. I love what I
trust. What do you love? As William
Shakespeare says: "There's The Rub" meaning
do you choose to live or to die, to sleep per
chance to dream? Or to live in this mortal
coil. So asks Hamlet.

To live.
To dream.
To teach.
Monkey.
My friends.
My squirrels.
Myself.

Always.

EPILOGUE

I think I found my eternal love for animals
when, at five years old, my dad caught a
little mouse in a trap in our garage. But she
did not die right away. Little Stella, I
called her. She was very hurt and she was
on her way. We found Stella mouse in the
trap and my dad got her out and I held her
in my little hands and then I put her in a
tiny box with a bed that I'd made from a
washcloth. And a tiny bowl of water. I sat
next to her, willing her to live. She didn't
though.

My little-girl-heart broke for the first
time. This was before the little birdy and
after my fear of Heaven.

So here's to you little Stella mouse. You
helped me find my heart. You are with me
always. I'm so
sorry we hurt you.
I've never hurt a
little mouse since.

And I promise I
never will.

    xx, Shelly

ACKNOWLEDGENTS

Thank you to Anthony Kafesjian for always having my back since 1999, and for answering the hard questions, solving the big problems, and always coming through with a bodily function joke.

Thank you to Ella Spice for your exquisite drawings that give life to my stories. Your vision, your generosity and your love are a gift that I could never repay.

Thank you to Nick Holmes for lighting a fire under my booty, and for inspiring me.

Thank you to Susan & Ted Ross and to Van Brooks for helping me find my path all those years ago.

Thank you to the Jenkins Family: Donnie, Duane, Dallas, Debbie, Donut & Doobie for all of the laughs, brotherhood and forever love.

Thank you to Jennie & Marcus Whitaker for providing the platform that made me finally commit to this. And to our Gilmore Family, especially the amazing Fans, that are the heart and soul of the family.

Thank you to the Pavillard Family for giving me a home.

Thank you Michael Dey, Christine Reed and The Afsharys for all that you do.

...and Randy, my first best friend.

Finally, to my Dad, who showed me that love is the home you intended for me. And Jack.